TRANSIT CHRONICLES

Nita's Story

Anita Brown Esq

DEDICATION

I dedicate this book to our youth in hopes that they will never accept limitations, whether self-imposed or from the outside world. It is my wish that they will pursue their dreams, use their gifts, come to know a higher power, seek true happiness, and one day realize the sheer joy that comes in helping to make others feel happy and whole.

ISBN: 9780986092817

TABLE OF CONTENTS

Acknowledgements

CHAPTER 1 – INTRODUCTION

Who on earth is Nita? Well, that would be me. I'm a chick hailing from East Orange, NJ. That's right – the land of Whitney & Dionne among others. Before reaching the golden age, THE BIG 50, I decided that it was time to embark upon Phase 2 of my life journey. This phase involves one of my greatest passions – writing.

I have always been a writer I suppose for as long as I have been a thinker. I have been a thinker since my kindergarten days which is when I first began to observe things in my immediate surroundings. In my high school days, these gifts of observation, thinking and writing manifested themselves into what one might call a supreme state of nerdhood. I hit the books HARD...so hard in fact, that I wound up being the valedictorian of my graduating class of 1983 at the infamous Clifford J. Scott H.S. It's not really infamous, but it sounds better when you say things like that, right?

Anyway, the supreme nerdhood did not stop in high school. At my undergraduate alma mater, the infamous – forget it. At Seton Hall University, I graduated magna cum laude & with the highest GPA in my major field of study. In the interest of full disclosure (I love that phrase & you'll probably see it again), you need to know that from my freshman year in HS through my graduation from SHU, I only received 2 C's (one in H.S. and one at SHU). It's a long story but not right now because eventually, you'll probably want to read this book. At least I hope so.

Before moving on, I should probably address the elephant in the room, which is that I am ABSOLUTELY & COMPLETELY addicted to the use of the ellipse. You know, these babies (...), the three dot wonders. I'm probably using them incorrectly more often than not, but I can't help myself. Sue me, they are my life. There, I said it...

Where was I? (you'll see this a lot, too). Oh yeah, after graduating from SHU, I took a year long break from school to 'find myself'- can't stand that phrase. Then, I entered Rutgers School of Law – Newark, in Newark, NJ. Here, my friends, is where the supreme nerdhood ended. I was simply not interested, very distracted and just not feeling it at all! I rarely read the case law, missed a few classes here and there and basically just phoned it in. This was in some ways tragic, because I knew as early as junior high school that I wanted to practice law. Some of the distractions included romance and a dormitory rodent infestation issue, but that's for another time because again, The Book, THE BOOK!

I did manage to complete law school and get my Juris Doctorate. However, passing the bar became somewhat of a career in and of itself. Apparently, I was completely cured of my nerdom. Nerdom, by the way, is a made up word. In addition to my addiction to ellipses, I tend to make up words. Even though there are almost a few hundred thousand words in the dictionary, I get bored easily. Although I am capable of speaking the King's English, I sometimes without warning shift into the use of massive slangery. It is simply who I am, so get used to it. Anyway, while attempting to pass the bar exam, I began substitute teaching for my old school district, and fell in love with the teaching profession.

Let me clarify before going on. The reason I explained my nerd beginnings was to point out that despite my love of books, words, studying and learning, I never really gave any thought to writing as a career goal or option. I never even considered

3

it a hobby or thought of sharing my musings with the outside, critical world. Nope, never!

Anyway (I say this a lot as well), while attempting to pass the bar exam I began substitute teaching in order to pay for the review courses and other things like food, clothing and shelter. Well, a funny thing happened on the way to being admitted to the NJ State Bar (which has yet to happen, but stay tuned). I developed a passion for teaching. It was actually a calling. Again, despite reigning as the Queen of Nerdom for decades, I had never considered teaching as a career either. Once, while interning at the A.C.L.U. during my Rutgers years, an elderly volunteer told me, "You'd make a great teacher, Anita." I immediately dismissed his remark as merely making conversation or as a not so subtle attempt to deter me from becoming an attorney. He must've been worried afterall, that I would make such a stellar and brilliant barrister, that I would easily overshadow his previous legal heroes and he simply couldn't have that.

Okay, two things – One, that last paragraph contained deplorable run-ons, among other things. A thousand pardons, but this and other serious grammar violations are unavoidable when

4

attempting to complete a thought in a book. Hopefully, none of my former English students will read this book. The second thing is that I have an extremely vivid, extremely overactive and sometimes frightening imagination. Again, it is simply who I am and you'll get used to it soon enough.

Anyway, short story long, I was well-received as a substitute teacher by students, teachers and parents alike (Yes, I made phone calls as a substitute teacher. House visits, too). The kids were amazed that I knew their names before noon, the teachers were amazed that the kids were well-behaved and had actually completed the work they left, and the parents praised me as well.

Ultimately, my school administrator suggested that I take the teacher exam to become licensed and certified. I took the exam and my career path was immediately clear to me. Bar exam, three tries and didn't pass it. Teacher exam, one take and I pass it. Bingo! Voila! The A.C.L.U. dude was right. I like to think of it all as divine intervention. Others might say it was de wine intervention, but that's for another book.

Where was I? Oh yes, I have been an educator for the past twenty years now. Now, this will sound vaguely familiar but even as an educator, I never gave any serious thought to writing professionally. Sure, I dabbled in poetry and song-writing here and there, and even went as far as copyrighting two collections of my assorted musings and ramblings. But a book? Nah!

As you have probably surmised by now, I tend to digress. Be loquacious. Long-winded. I talk way too much and get off track. I'm doing it right now. Many will tell you that I do this to the point of aggravation and that my excessive chatter could very easily lead to violent outbursts and pleadings for me to cease talking. In some ways, it is a curse that has plagued me since my youth. Sadly, there is no cure for it. One must simply endure it for the duration. I merely offer this tidbit as a precaution of sorts. This is essentially your last chance to escape the contents of this book, and all its sordid twists and turns. Don't say you weren't warned!

Let me cut to the chase (digressors always say that). Introductions are supposed to give some insight into why the author wrote his or her book in the first place. Well, many events, encounters and circumstances led me to pen this story. Most of these center around me indulging my passions on the internet (music, poetry, sports, Star Trek etc.). I joined groups centered around these interests and forged many online friendships as a result. I began to freely express myself – thoughts, opinions, feelings, humor.

For example, I became a huge Frank Sinatra fan during the time that I was taking care of my grandmother in the early 2000s. NANA was stricken with Alzheimer's Disease and listening to Sinatra's music and watching his films and shows allowed her to hold onto something as her memory declined. I joined one online group called The-Voice, headed by my dear friend, Rick Apt and the positive feedback I received from them about my Sinatra poems, parody songs and a fan website led me to copyright my first collection of poems and songs covering various topics…

More recently, I joined another online page for gospel singer, Bebe Winans and made friends there as well. I found his music and artistry to be quite inspirational and attended a few of his concerts and appearances. Bebe actually wrote his first book at the age of 49 and no, I did not decide I wanted to write my book then (still had my car) but I did copyright more poetry and songs. The collection includes 47 songs and poems. I was 47 years old at the time. (I have a thing with numbers, but I don't really have time to get into that right now)…

Ok, I'm almost done with this intro. The thing that really led to me writing this book was a shift in career. I left classroom teaching and teacher mentoring to concentrate on tutoring. I must admit that I had become somewhat disenchanted with the educational system. The manner in which teachers are expected and required to teach (or not teach) does little, in my opinion to educate, enlighten, empower or even prepare our children for the world beyond their classroom doors (but that's another book).

Anyway, I knew this shift from school district teaching to tutoring would involve a drastic salary cut and I prepared in advance. I'm a planner, preparer – the thinker, observer thingy again. First I downsized from a one-bedroom to a studio apartment. About a year later, I decided it would be better to sell my car for the payoff price and start taking the bus again. Luckily, I was never a slave to an automobile. I was an avid bike rider, walker or bus rider when necessary. I was 40 when I purchased my first car, and that was only to be able to check on my Nana who had to be placed in a nursing home during her last days battling Alzheimer's. Biking and busing at night through bad weather wasn't practical or wise, so I got my first car, a Nissan Sentra. I've had a couple of others since then and sold my last car, a Honda CR-V in September of 2012 and began taking the bus.

I knew immediately that riding the bus again was going to be quite the adventure. All the memories of my previous bus riding came flooding back in dramatic, traumatic and nightmarish fashion. I began documenting my bizarre happenings on Facebook, titling them the "Transit Chronicles". Facebook friends were often amused by my daily misery and remarked 'You should write a book.'

Finally, after a severe reduction in tutoring assignments, I was forced to give up my apartment and move in with my twin sister's family. I am extremely grateful to her, but I'm the loner type, having lived alone for some 20 years. The summer of 2014 was going to be a long hot one, so I decided that now is as good a time as any to write this book. So, I finally and formally invite you to brace yourselves and turn the page....

CHAPTER 2 – WHERE DO I SIT?

As I have mentioned before, I am the planning type. This didn't change when I made my triumphant return to riding the bus. Remnants of my nerdom still linger and I tend to analyze, overanalyze, organize and compartmentalize regular everyday tasks that most normal human beings carry out with little or no thought. Surely, you know by now that I am far from normal and my choices and decisions are usually the result of much calculation, pomp and circumstance. I can't just get on the bus, take a seat and enjoy the ride. Nope. I had to plan where I would be sitting and why. Who, I ask you, anticipates well in advance of the bus' arrival what seat to pick and then runs through in their head, the various scenarios that might unfold in the event of the wrong seat choice? Well, I do. Unfortunately, I learned soon enough that it didn't matter where I sat, because I seem to have or be, a magnet for THE BIZARRE!

Case in point (strange phrase), on one of my very first post-auto rides, I opted to sit in the front of the bus. I don't really care for those long, three-seater deals in the front of the bus, but I recalled that shady things tend to happen in the very back of the bus (transit or Greyhounds). Also, the males usually gravitate to the back of the bus, and I always get the side eye from my older bus-riding colleagues and church going brethren, as if the fast track to hell could be found right in the back of the bus. True story. This really happens. They seem to be saying with their judgmental eyes 'There are perfectly good seats up front, so why are you heading to the back, you brazen hussy?! For shaaame!' They had me pegged for a woman of loose morals simply because I opted to be incogneeta in the back of the bus for crying out loud (wonderful phrase)! If any of you busy-bodies are reading this, I want you to know that I take great umbrage, GREAT UMBRAGE at your accusatory stares and grunts. Hmmph! There's really no winning on these public buses I tell ya!

Where was I? Oh yeah, I'm sitting on the 3-seater deal in the front part of the bus. I need to stress that it is VERY important to know whether to sit on one of the end seats or in the middle seat. It seems like a no-brainer to opt for the end seat, but not so fast. It all depends on who is boarding after you. This is frightening because it is something over which I have zero control. Planners need control. I felt immediately vulnerable, but because I was holding up the passengers behind me and also because I quickly spotted some undesirables near both empty end seats, I hastily plopped down in the middle seat. My regret was instantaneous. I had made a colossal mistake!

There was a time in my life, albeit brief, that I was not utterly disgusted by direct contact from complete strangers in public places. I was actually okay with sitting down next to someone whose thigh or arm rested temporarily against mine. Well, this was not the case anymore. I have watched too many television shows that inform us of the many germs that we all carry, transfer and share in public places, in close quarters. There is also the fact that some folks just look and smell...well, Nasty! 100% EWWW! Am I wrong to want no parts of them? Am I???

No sooner had I taken my middle seat, when a rather portly fellow decided to take the end seat to my left. Not only did he physically squeeze in and shove me over to the other end seat, leaving me dangerously close to Undesirable#1, but his essence was most unpleasant. I mean, he WREAKED of the undead and the dead, or worse. It was the kind of smell that aids new dieters, because once you get a whiff of the stench, eating was the furthest thing from your mind.

Don't get me wrong. Anyone of any size can smell bad, and there are some health conditions that have the unfortunate and unavoidable side effect of bad odor, but this young man was simply messy, and unclean. Yuck. Unfortunately, his ample girth rendered me paralyzed, unable to move or breathe much at all. I had to wait until he exited the bus. My prayers were answered after about 5 excruciating, torturous minutes and he got up to disembark. My misery would soon be over, or so I thought…

Do you know what this character had the nerve to do? As he was walking to the front, he shook his head, held his nose and said "Whew, somebody stinks!" Then he turned and looked back in my direction as if to say 'it's her'. And do you know that the entire front half of the bus fixed their gaze on me, co-conspirators in his bold-faced lie! Oh sure, shift the blame to little old me. HOW DARE HE! (love this phrase). I felt even more betrayed, however, by my fellow bus riders who had cosigned his shenanigans. I had planned on us having marvelous comradery on our rides to and fro. I actually envisioned us singing songs, sharing family photos, the whole bit. Well, they can forget that now. Big Boy had ruined it with his da-stinked (not distinct) odor. Unreal!

Needless to say, the next time out, I fought off the judgmental stares and headed straight to the back of the bus. It was nothing like I expected. There were no loud, vulgar, cursing teens, no strange odors and no unexplained stains on the seats or floor like I remembered in the past. I almost broke into a public smile at the thought of my first transit victory. Sadly, my enthusiasm was short-lived because I noticed a 'gentleman' staring straight at me. I mean he was just boring a hole through my soul with his eyes!

It is 2015 and everyone should know the 5-second stare rule. It is universally understood in all corners of this nation, if not of the world. Looking, staring, gazing, glancing or peeking at someone for more than 5 seconds borders on rudeness, nosiness, stalkation or overt threat territory. Most civilized straphangers know this. This gentleman was obviously nowhere in the vicinity of civilized and he continued to ogle me shamelessly. I immediately employed my usually reliable counter-stare moves – the exaggerated eye rolling, the loud huff-and-puff sounds and the hard to miss, full quarter body turn in the opposite direction – all to no avail. After one last vicious glare by yours truly, the offensive ogler says "Don't you have a twin sister? Y'all went to Scott, right?" Right about here is where I insert the Homer Simpson 'Dolp!'

I cannot tell you how many times that I have hatefully glared down curious starers on the bus, only to discover that they were former students, neighbors, classmates or church friends. It is quite embarrassing. This particular situational development was no less uncomfortable and I stumbled over my words to say "Oh, oh yeah. Heyyy. How've ya been?" And still no clue as to who he might be. Shhheeesh. I was feeling so guilty for coming off as either too good, or unapproachable and all kindsa transit snobby.

Then all of a sudden, homeboy felt comfortable enough to pull out a brown paper bag containing a very tall can of beer. Now, mind you, it was not yet noon and I still only had a vague memory of him from our school days. I'm not even sure if I even liked him when we were in school. Luckily, I planned for these kind of situations too and I promptly exited the bus two stops earlier than I needed to. I could not after all, run the risk that he might ask me for my number to get reacquainted or even worse, follow me off the bus to offer me some of his brew or God knows what else. It's not like this sort of thing hasn't happened before. True story. I'm a magnet I tell ya...for all manner of humanity. A MAGNET!

There are only a couple of other things I need to say about seating choices and situations. First of all, there is no worse feeling than to sit down on the bus and find that a recently vacated seat is extremely warm. The heat is not from some advanced heating mechanism provided by a caring transit authority. No, it is coming from the hind parts/regions of a fellow straphanger. Ewww! I have NO desire to mingle with the warm vestiges of some stranger's posterior. It's some sort of sick, forced intimacy. You are now ONE with God knows who and this is certainly not what they mean by hot cross buns. Nuff said...

The other thing that I must mention is that it is imperative that once you take your seat, you do NOT get involved in any way, shape or form with the seating choices and behaviors of anyone else. Period! I have often caught myself glaring at passengers who failed to give up a seat for an elderly or handicapped rider. I've caught myself frowning disgustedly at women who board the bus with unruly children and seat them next to an unfortunate rider who must endure their crying, screaming, spoiled brat who is in the midst of a major tantrum. How much more considerate it would have been if the parents had sat in the middle as a buffer, so their fellow passengers didn't have to endure this little rascal's tomfoolery. Too much!

Keep in mind that none of this directly affected me or was any of my business. The very last straw I think was when I looked up at the precise moment that a woman sat in one of those three-seater deals and sat all the way back EVEN THOUGH she had an infant strapped to her back in one of those modern, convenient carrying contraptions. I was heart attack horrified and almost let out a primal scream. Luckily others had seen it too and informed or reminded her that her baby was on her back. She had the nerve to give a nonchalant chuckle and only moved forward a few inches!

That was it. I had seen enough. I needed to just mind my own business. I would no longer, under any circumstances, look up once I was seated. I would make no eye contact...not even with the bus driver. It was just too much of a risk. My sanity was escaping a little bit per each bus ride. I was just going to look down. Yes, DOWN is the safest.

CHAPTER 3 – NO SEATS! (SRO)

There is certainly no way that I can chronicle the transit experience without covering the abysmal scenario of boarding a bus that has no seats left. It is one of the most nerve-racking, unbearable situations that straphangers must face. I'm not talking about inconsiderate, selfish folks who put their packages, pocketbooks, feet or tiny babies in a seat they didn't pay for and begrudgingly move the aforementioned when you ask. I'm talking about when there are absolutely no available seats.

Being forced to stand on a packed bus is the lowest of lows for the transit rider. It is an insufferable, dignity-stealing affair. Now, keep in mind that each and every one of us commuters has been both a sitter and a stander at some point. Yet, you would not believe the attitude and personality switch that occurs when one goes from a stander to a sitter, and vice versa. I mean, God forbid you are standing and your jacket or bag brushes up against one of the sainted sitters. Ohhh, the disdain on their countenance. They know very well how maniacally the bus drivers drive when they are commandeering a crowded bus. These lunatics at the wheel leave you little control over your own balance, let alone your belongings. Heaven help you if you accidentally step on or brush against a sitter's foot. You would think they had been spat upon. Give me a break! We're in this together. Aren't we???

I suppose it's just human nature. It's that damnable sense of entitlement. It's quite similar to the driver, turned pedestrian switcheroo. When you're driving a car and pedestrians are taking their sweet time crossing an intersection, or walking in the street instead of on the sidewalk, you don't hesitate to give them the angry horn. You feel like saying, 'Yeah I see you, as in I.C.U. is where you're gonna wind up if you make me miss this turn!' You become livid enough to want to tap them a bit, or help them donate a few teeth to science. Or is that just me? Yet, when you're suddenly a pedestrian, something inside of you says 'slow down' and you glare at the driver as if to say 'You bet'not hit me!'

Similarly, if you're driving and stopped at a light near a bus stop, you sometimes think 'Wow, look at some of these characters.' However, if you're waiting for the bus, you resent the driving public gawking at you. You want to shout out 'Never saw anyone catch a bus before?!!', but lashing out in such a manner would cause you to lose sanity points with your fellow straphangers. You really don't want them to think you're of unsound mind. No, that would be awful. Yet, we act this way and it really is madness when you think about it. Truth be told, we commuters (whether on foot or behind the wheel) are quite the condescending and hypocritical bunch. Sigh.

Where was I? Oh yeah. In the interest of full disclosure, I must admit that I, too sometimes adopt a pompous attitude as a sitter. In my defense, I should say that even when I'm an arrogant sitter, I don't get mad at swaying bags and purses (maybe dripping umbrellas, though) as much as I do when someone parks his or her personage in a most awkward spot. I would appreciate it if my commuting comrades would be careful not to stand in a way that situates their parts right at my eye level. Is it too much to ask that they shuffle their feet so that neither of us is embarrassed? For the sake of decency, I only ask that you not make me privy to your privates. I'm just not that kind of woman.

Another major source of angst and aggravation in the SRO scenario is when folks refuse to move towards the back of a bus that is quickly becoming packed and crowded. I don't recall what the maximum amount of standees by law is, but I am certain that the majority of buses are regularly in violation. It is neither safe, nor fair to keep packing us onto this metal monstrosity. Trouble inevitably rear its ugly head. Unfortunately, I doubt the drivers undergo a psych exam that measures their sadistic tendencies, so it is incumbent upon us straphangers to cooperate. Yes, we have entered pickpocket and cheap thrills territory, but until we can do something about it, MOVE BACK, YOU IDIOTS!!!

I don't like to resort to name-calling, but my comrades can be pretty unreasonable at times, and often downright irrational. There is no guarantee of comfort or decency on these bus rides. Expectations are low. Forget that whole 'public service' jazz you hear and read about. It is a thing of the past. Long and short of it is that some of us have places to be – work, home, school, court, whatever. How dare you hold up the entire bus because you don't feel like moving back to let others on. You're not going to miss your stop if you're loud and pushy enough. Some of them seem to be waiting for clues or special signals from GOD or maybe from another planet. I repeat, MOOOOOVE!!!!

It is one of the most frustrating situations that can easily lead to bus rage. Oh yes, bus rage is a real phenomenon and can be as lethal as road rage. I have seen shoving matches and heard vile, filthy, profane exchanges and threats, all to no avail. I've even seen some of these stubborn folks followed off of the bus. I've often wondered if fisticuffs ever ensued. I'm not a proponent of violence but these agents of delay are pushing it! I, myself try to move back whenever possible and try not to get involved beyond a menacing stare or look of total disgust.

More SRO drama ensues when folks try to leave a packed bus and some rude boarders rush onto the bus before they can even get out. You have to squeeze, shove, punch or push your way off of this prison on wheels. Is it too much for the driver to say "Coming out."? Apparently, sometimes it is. These morons are obviously just barely keeping a lid on the pressure cooker that is public transportation. Again, we must rely on one another, so hold your horses, boarders! Let your long-suffering standee comrades off the bus or we'll be faced with another 'I'm not moving' scenario. Stubbornness has absolutely no place on a public bus. Time is always of the essence.

There are some things that are always annoying whether a bus is packed or not. Then there are other things that become even more unbearable when on a packed bus. One of those things is farebeaters. Yyyyyesss. THEM! They march up those three steps knowing full well they have no money and no intention of paying the fare. They have no shame and no guilt about holding up the lives of folks who paid their fares without incident, story or excuse. Their excuses are so weak and pathetic and then they have the unmitigated gall to get an attitude when the driver stops them.

Normally, I'm on the side of the rider – it is in the 2014-2015 Commuter Code, Chapter 7, page 38, section 4. No, really. However, as a standee on an SRO bus, my feet, legs, arms, fingers and even my eyes are tired! Even the sitters are aggravated. ENOUGH! PAY or GET OFF!!!

Well, do you know that the control freak, tyrant of a transit driver will actually stop the bus cold?! In a loud voice, he asserts his authority and tells the farebeater, beggar, or unfortunate sap (whatever you choose to call them) that he or she must either put their fare in or get off, or the cops will be called to escort him or her out. This of course, immediately leads to angry yelling and shouting from all parties - standees, sitters, adults, children, everyone. What an uncivilized lot we are.

Usually, the situation resolves itself when some kind or annoyed rider is able to reach his pockets in this crowded deathtrap and pay the person's fare, which was probably the farebeater's intent all along. Sure, no one is really hurt, but lives and outlooks have been forever altered as a result. It's just not right I tell you.

SRO buses are sinister. They make us hypocrites. Sitters vs. standers. Also, people already on the bus vs. people who want to get on the bus. How many times have I been on a bus and become livid each time the driver stops to let someone on? I'm ashamed to say. Secretly, I am cursing him six ways to Sunday and I don't care that it's raining or snowing and that these people need to get on the bus, too. At the same time, you get a tinge of anger and guilt when the driver doesn't stop for an elderly or handicapped person who is clearly flagging the bus down. The truth of the matter is that deep down, even though you know it's wrong and it could be you that is one day passed by, you make peace with it. It is hypocrisy at its ugliest, and you're not proud of it, but you are happy that the bus is still moving and the rest of the world be damned!

I guess I should note that crowded buses are not always a bad thing. Why? Because they have afforded me great opportunities to witness human nature in its rawest form. I have noticed for example that bus riding tends to foster wanton profanity, rage and hooliganism – and this from otherwise law-abiding citizens. It is really quite frightening how easily one adopts these behaviors and deems them acceptable.

I find myself angry even before I actually board the bus. I glare at the riders with huge bags or baby strollers. I glare at the wheelchair passengers, not because of their handicap, but because some of the allegedly well-trained drivers make it a project and take ten minutes or more to situate our hoveround homies. I glare at the loud, obnoxious teenage riders. I glare at the riders having loud cell phone conversations. I glare at the church crowd who seem to be calling us heathens with their eyes. I glare at the grown men and women who have probably been riding buses all their lives but have still not mastered how to slide a bill into the fare machine slot (why don't they iron or flatten out their money instead of coming on board with their stale, old, crinkled up dollar bills that they know will cause us to lose precious minutes?). Unbelievable! Yes, the transit system does much to ensure great business for eye doctors and anger management therapists.

One last SRO pet peeve situation I must mention is when some moron boards the bus with a huge bill, looking for change. REALLY?!! No, we don't have change! First of all, we are too tightly packed in to even get to our purses and wallets to see if we have change. Secondly, are you serious?! You had plenty of time to get change from the store you were standing in front of before this late, crowded bus even arrived. Thirdly, if we had that kind of change, don't you think we might've opted for a cab instead of this state-sanctioned masochistic motorcade?! At this point, even if I had change, I would not tell you or give it to you as a matter of principle. Hmmph, the nerve!

CHAPTER 4 – ROMANCE ON THE RAILS

It never ceases to amaze me just how candid, detailed, generous and downright TMI folks can be in sharing their personal relationship details and other intimate, delicate, sensitive, embarrassing information when commuting via public transportation. I mean there are things I wouldn't share with my own twin, let alone broadcast to perfect strangers on a bus! Who does that?! And yet, the buses have somehow become the TMZ of the transit system. This is a small world indeed and if there's anything you need to know about anyone, then by all means board a bus. It's better than Twitter, Youtube and Instagram combined. No exaggeration.

Case in point – I hopped on a bus on my way to work one day and sat behind someone that seemed relatively safe, normal, sane. WRONG! Obviously my people and character judging skills are slipping because this heretofore quiet, unassuming woman answered her phone and began to tell quite a tale. It seems that she had been having trouble with the mother of her son's children (her grandchildren). This would-be daughter-in-law apparently did not have the decency to get up in time to get the children off to school or to even fix breakfast for the little darlings. These tasks were thrust upon this sweet grandmother who, upon closer whiff, smelled of a brewery (again this is early morning).

Happily, I can report that on that day, things were different. The grandmother told her phonemate, "Yeah chile, she was over bright and early, fed the kids, then walked them to school" (lets out loud, uncouth laugh). She then goes on to say that she called her son repeatedly about this issue and he must've finally told her. She says "Whatever he told her must've worked" After another unsettling guffaw, her equally loud phonemate said "Oh, is he out?!" and the grandma replied, "No, not yet but he gonna get transferred to a less restricted section soon and then he'll have regular phone privileges." I'm certain that my mouth must've stayed wide open for a full 10 seconds. Yep, that last remark explained it all! You just can't make this stuff up!

Another time a young, starry eyed, cheerful chap got on the bus, followed by a young woman and others he apparently knew. He says hello to the young lady and she doesn't even pretend to feign enthusiasm of any sort. She offers a very weak 'Hello', but she did engage in a brief, polite conversation and things seemed to be going well. I was beginning to have hope that romance was not dead at all and was happy for the guy when out of nowhere the young Romeo says to his would-be Juliet, "I was wondering if I could have your number again?" I'm sure everyone in earshot wanted to yell out 'Noooo!' and 'Whyyyy?' It was going so well, but it was too late. We tried to avert our eyes from what was sure to be a humiliating exchange, but each of us collectively leaned a little forward because we wanted to hear this. We were shamelessly and voyeuristically involving ourselves in this young man's affairs, but we couldn't help it. We had to know.

We were floored by her response. She said, with her cell phone in full view "Oh, I don't use my phone anymore". We were obviously more stunned than this poor simpleton, because he proceeded to twist the knife into his own back and asked "Oh, you don't use it anymore?" She responded with a quick, "No". We were like "Oh no she didn't!" Meanwhile, it looked as if he was going to say something else. Luckily, he pressed the button and exited at the next stop with nary a word uttered. How do these poor souls make it through life in this cruel, wicked world? Even more amazing though, is how I managed to keep from laughing out loud when her phone rang. I was sitting right next to them. Romance on the rails can be humorous and tragic all at once.

Some of Cupid's other commuters have less than catastrophic experiences wooing their sweeties. The successful ones oddly enough are very bold. One guy on my morning commute would exit at my bus stop, kissing a girl goodbye and not 3 seconds later, another girl would appear smooching and sitting much too close if you ask me. They were like mating St. Bernards! Did it not occur to him that one day Chick #2 might arrive early to the bus stop and catch him bidding Chick #1 a fond adieu? Or Chick #1 would see him smooching Chick #2 after swearing she was the only one for him? BOLD!

Now, these love or lust-tinged encounters were not always the most pleasant or beautiful displays of romance. Sometimes, things got downright ugly. Some of my commuting comrades air their dirty laundry with frightening candor and brutal realism. There was one couple that entered the bus cussing and fussing, sat down cussing and fussing and finally exited, cussing and fussing. These are the types that you leave off of your invite lists – parties, weddings, and other gatherings. Sadly, you cannot keep them off of the bus. Their argument seemed to be about the woman's sister. She thought her mate's brotherly love towards her sister needed to be a little bit more brotherly and a lot less lovey. He said "Why the ....would I be sweatin' your sister like that?!" and she shot back, "Das what I wanna know....!" She was seething and frankly I was hoping he could come up with a good answer for all of our sakes. No such luck.

This jerk made the pivotal mistake of comparing and making analogies. He brings up some old male neighbor of theirs and tells her he never made a big deal of how extra nice she is to him. Idiot. She yells in a voice loud enough to be heard underground "Mr. Tolliver is blind and in a wheelchair, stupid....! It's not the same!" Then she adds, "Das okay, I got something for you". Ummm, these are code words for impending violence. He missed them completely...

He says, "...... what's that supposed to mean? You trippin. I'm supposed to be scared....!" and she says, way too calmly, "Don't even worry about it". Needless to say I was scared. And I am not exaggerating in the least when I say, he should be VERY worried, every waking moment (and every sleeping moment, too). What an idiot. Quit while you are behind and for the love of God, stay away frrom her sister!

Another rail romance you witness on the bus is what I call, the 'first of the month' couples. This is when the baby daddys, who didn't have the decency to make honest women of the mothers of their children, will magically appear at the mother's side at the beginning of the month when she receives a public assistance check. Mind you, she is probably on public assistance in the first place because the baby daddy offers little financial help and yet, here he is trying to get some of the money.

It all starts out as a picture of romantic bliss and familial harmony. All are smiling. They have food and packages. All is bliss. Then, this shameless joker gets greedy and comes up with some pitiful story that starts with, "Can you let me hold...?" It all spirals downward very quickly into an all-out verbal war. Before he even finishes his lame story, she is hurling the most vile insults and telling him what she really feels about him deep down. I mean, deep deep down! If you are ever seated near one of these couples and you hear that phrase, "Can you let me hold?...", do not even wait for him to finish or for her to reply. Move immediately because anyone within a four-seat radius is in grave, grave danger! Not only will your ears be damaged permanently by the volume and vulgarity, but you could be injured by flying objects, fists or elbows. It's very easy to become an injured innocent bystander on the bus.

Sometimes the conversations become very juvenile. One guy was arguing about her not getting the kind of cookie he asked for. She goes off into a tirade about the money being for her kids to eat, etc and not about him. He counters with "Well last time you said you were gonna get me the Chip Ahoys, but you got them stupid rainbow sprinkled ones because they were on sale. And you said this time, you'd get em." She yells, "That was before you had me to get that stupid cereal you like. And don't forget the shake I got you at McDonald's. This money gotta last!" He responds "How it's gonna last if you getting your nails and hair done?" She fires back "Oh, I can't look good just because I got a no-good baby daddy who don't care about nothing but himself?!" I had to get off the bus before they finished the conversation, but it was certainly spiraling out of control.

Another guy tried to reason with the mother of his children. " But I need it to pay the insurance for the car. Don't you want me to pick y'all up? Or you'd rather ride the bus there?" Big mistake – "EXCUSE ME?!", she said. "When the last time you ever picked us up in your car?" (His silence here is good, because it's a rhetorical question). She continues, "Please, last time I even saw you with your car, you was riding some ….. and it wasn't even your wife!" YOWZA! I can't. I just can't.

Another troubling situation that falls under the love and romance on the rails department is the 'hot chick syndrome'. Guys consider any chick who is scantily, shamelessly or barely clad a 'hot chick'. She could be a PYT or just physically beautiful. I have also observed that most men riding the bus (or in general) will find any woman other than the one they happen to be with at the moment, to be of the 'hot chick' variety. Men will trip over their feet trying to have some kind of interaction with said hot chick. These guys will practically knock over a senior citizen, child, disabled or pregnant person to offer up their seat to one. The hot chick will giggle excessively, much to the chagrin of the angry resentful mate . This is where troubling situations arise…

I once saw a guy who remained seated while three women (one with bags, the other with kids and another elderly woman) without seats, stood up around him. When a woman in a dress two sizes too small got on the bus, this same guy made an utter fool of himself offering this bagless, childless, able-bodied hussy aka hot chick his seat. He even put his hand out to prevent the other women from getting the seat before she got to it. This is what I call selective chivalry. It's not right.

How do I know it's not right? Because the woman with whom the man boarded the bus, seated right next to him, made it clear that it was not right. She was actually around the same age as the alleged hot chick and better looking if you ask me, but when that fool stood up to give this hot chick his seat, she let loose with such a deadly, cold gaze that the hot chick stopped in her tracks and said, "That's okay. Thank you anyway". Wise decision. How dare he!

I often wonder what happens when these battling couples get home, but sometimes you don't have to wonder. Another simpleton whose testosterone got the better of him tried to offer his seat to another hot chick type. His woman quickly made her feelings known. "Oh, I don't think so.

What, you want that …..?! I guess you got some place else to sleep tonight, huh? Kill me! All of a sudden you a gentleman! Sitcho … down!" I leave out the cusses, but you get the gist. And he did, too.

In closing, I guess what I have learned in all of this is that the bus is simply no place for love and romance. Don't try to seek it there. Don't try to keep it there. Don't try to express it there. Just try to stay focused on arriving safely to your destination without putting yourself and other straphangers in danger. Just do what I do – LOOK DOWN at all times until your stop comes up.

CHAPTER 5 – BUS STOP SHENANIGANS

You won't believe this, but ON the bus itself is not the only place you will encounter the madness and insanity that is commuting. You will find yourself privy to the oddities of transit life before you even board the bus. In fact, I can't tell you how much life and sheer lunacy I have witnessed while waiting on my commuter chariot.

The first thing I realized is that there are not nearly enough benches and bus shelters available. Depending on what area you live in, you can be in serious trouble when the wintry, stormy weather rolls around. In my own neck of the woods, I have counted maybe one bench every 6 to 7 bus stops. I should say bus shelters. An actual bench at a shelter is quite the luxury in this corner of the world. I use the term 'shelter' very loosely because these contraptions are barely two people deep and I wouldn't suggest trying to squeeze into an already crowded shelter either. Things could take a violent turn. You're better off taking your chances with nature's fury than with the wrath of a commuter caught in precipitation of any kind. You will quickly find yourself on the short end of the bus rage I mentioned. It's not pretty, but again you learn to live with it.

The next thing I realized about bus stops is that they aren't really for those actually waiting for a bus. If you are lucky enough to spot a shelter with seats, the seats are usually taken over by non-commuters. Modern day squatters is what they are and they have essentially hijacked seats from the paying, bus-riding public. It ain't riiight-TA! These characters even have the nerve to save seats for their loitering friends. Unbelievable, right?

Just who are these bench-jackers? Teenagers, the mentally ill, the TADDs (I'll explain later), weedheads, drunks, religious zealots, the homeless and your average run-of-the-mill vagrants and other miscreants. These folks will hit you with the serious side-eye if you even look like you're approaching an empty seat. Every now and then, when I'm feeling bold and extremely tired, I ignore my inner voice that is screaming "Danger!" and grab a seat. It doesn't happen often though.

Sitting down is not always a good thing. Why? Because you run the risk of human interaction. I'm not sure if I mentioned this before, but I'm seriously considering a facelift. It's not because I'm terribly unhappy with the attributes the good Lord has seen fit to bless me with. It's just that I seem to have the type of face that makes total strangers feel comfortable telling me their complete life story (from conception to present). I mean they share every nauseating, uncomfortable detail. Who knew a bus stop could morph into a torture chamber? I hear about family drama, incarcerations, money matters, sexcapades – you name it, they share it!

Before I go on, let me explain the difference between 'mentally ill' and 'TADD'. Mentally ill folks are just that – people with a mental illness that keeps them from functioning 'fully' in school, work or life in general. Why anyone would want to fully participate in this wacky world, if they had a good excuse not to, is beyond me. Anyway, I completely get mentally ill folks because I am the daughter of a woman who is mentally ill, which is why I was raised by my grandmother, but I'm digressing again. Mentally ill folks sit on bus stop benches just to pass time. They may giggle or stare or ask for spare change but they're essentially harmless. Nine times out of ten, their bark is worse than their bite.

TADDs on the other hand are very problematic. Their bite and bark are scary. TADD stands for - The Absolutely Diabolically Deranged. There are countless TADDs roaming the streets freely and taking up residence at some of the bus stops. They may be certifiably insane and criminally so. OR, they may be undiagnosed and mingling amongst us uninformed folks who walk around completely oblivious to the undercurrent of rage and violence lying dormant. Be afraid. Be very afraid.

Seriously though, I have discovered that TADDs love bus stops. They find one and essentially take it over. There is one woman in town who visits and frequents various bus stops. She glares menacingly at everyone and literally growls and snarls at you. If these tactics aren't enough to get you to back away or give up the notion of sitting down, she has been known to spit in the direction of unsuspecting commuters.

I've decided to call her Jane. I'm not sure why, but it seems to fit. She is just downright hateful and evil. They need to put her picture up with a warning at all bus stops, but I'm afraid she would just rip it down. I learned early on to pick and choose my transit battles. I don't care how tired I am, I will not sit down next to her at the bus stop. I don't really know why, but she absolutely terrifies me. Sometimes, she actually rides the bus to the other side of town, but that scenario is too horrifying to go into (maybe in my next book).

Jane's TADD status is readily apparent from her unclean, seasonably inappropriate wardrobe to her unclean, physical appearance, not to mention her vile language and snarling. I came across another bench-jacker whose TADD status was not so easily detectible. He was quiet, neatly dressed, and hygienically sound in appearance etc. Once I sat down however, he jumped up abruptly, started to walk away and then just as suddenly turned back to scream at me, "HEY! HOW COME YOU'RE WEARING PURPLE?! WHO TOLD YOU TO WEAR PURPLE?! DID YOU PAY FOR THAT?!!"

At first, I just froze. It was so unexpected. He stood there waiting for my response. Luckily, I've learned a few things since I've been hopping buses. One, if a TADD has a bible in their hands and this guy did, proceed with extreme caution. I remember two evangelists who used to preach hell and damnation with great fury at a Main Street bus stop when I was much younger. They thumped their bibles frequently and preached loudly but for the most part they stuck to The Word and made a lot of sense. I'm no A student of Bible Study, but I simply do not recall any scripture about the color purple being a sin.

Second thing I've learned is that you must meet TADD with equally TADD-like behavior (i.e. oh yeah, I'll show ya deranged, buddy!). I mentioned my dear, sainted grandmother NANA, who was old school, God-fearing, had high expectations, made you be still if someone had passed away, and didn't allow smoking, drinking, swearing or telling dirty jokes. Well, the vile, filthy tirade of guttural language complete with flailing arms and evil facial scowls that I unleashed on this TADD would've broken my grandmother's heart. She must've been rolling over in her sweet little corner of heaven if she heard me. However, even she would understand that drastic situations call for drastic measures and until they come up with an effective TADD-repellant spray, a commuter has to do what a commuter has to do. Forgive me, Nana…

Oh, and if you want to get technical, I wasn't even wearing anything purple. He must've been referring to my book bag in which I lug all my work and worldly possessions. That book bag was magenta, not purple. Anyone who knows me, knows that I'm an incurable matchaholic and misidentifying or mismatching a color is inexcusable. He's lucky I didn't go off on Him…

well, even more than I already had. Bottom line is, it worked. He kept walking and didn't bother me anymore. So there!

Once I came upon a woman at a bus stop, bible in tow, and she was giving an impassioned sermon about avoiding the ills and evils of this world and turning your life over to Jesus. I consider myself a Believer and a Christian, so I smiled as I listened to her. Unfortunately, a young man passing by accidentally bumped her, causing her bible to fall. The profanity that escaped this woman's lips almost rivaled my own TADD defense tirade. I was dumbfounded. To make matters worse, she bent down to pick up her bible, and a few lottery tickets fell out. So much for the ills and evils of this world. Truth really is stranger than fiction. You can't make this kinda stuff up!

Okay, let me get back to the 'life story' folks. Having a kind, simple, friendly type face can be both a blessing and a curse. I don't mind being kind to strangers and exchanging pleasantries at a bus stop, but there is something about my countenance that makes folks unburden their souls to me right then and there. Who does that? Well, you'd be surprised…

One day a man sits down next to me at the bus stop right outside of the local hospital and proceeds to tell me about a surgery he had that left him unable to perform his manly duties. I kid you not, and I'm paraphrasing in order to spare you the language and phrases he actually used. If that wasn't enough, he went on to talk about his sordid love life and how he realized now how much of a jerk he was in his dealings with women. He even managed to slip in the fact that he was married and these scandalous rendezvous had occurred during the marriage. All the while I'm thinking, where is that bus??

No bus. So Don Juan continues and tells me about the time he was in the hallway with a neighbor, and then on the roof of his workplace, and in the Shop Rite parking lot. He once had an intimate encounter in a hospital while visiting a friend there. I think he actually was looking for sympathy because he could no longer do the dirty deed. I almost fell out of my seat when he said his wife was so loyal and he loved her. She should've been hearing this mess, not me!

Pretending not to listen didn't stop this clown from going on and on with his shameful shenanigans. I did my best not to make any eye contact and just nodded my head. I didn't offer up one word however, because I might have accidentally let him know what I really thought about his tomfoolery. Afterall, he could've been a TADD, so I just kept praying the bus would come and I could escape this torturous tale.

Another time, a woman at the bus stop told me she was a twin. I admit that I only listened because she was a twin. I'm a sucker for all things twin. It's a twin thing. I can't explain it, but it was a big mistake in this case. She told me about the dilemma her family faced in trying to get a relative buried. She said she called the deceased her brother, but he wasn't her real brother. He was a cousin that her parents raised. There was a money issue (isn't there always?) because he was too young to get money left to him and the money somehow disappeared (doesn't it always?) He was mad, moved to another state and considered a group of his friends his real family, blah blah blah. Well, he died unexpectedly, and now a bunch of different people were trying to claim his body - his friends, his real mother's sister, her family etc. - What she was worried about was that he would wind up in Potter's Field if they couldn't agree on who would claim him and take care of his funeral.

I sometimes have an out of body experience while listening to life stories, meaning I am hovering above the situation and saying to myself 'I cannot believe she is telling me all of this!' What goes ON in this world?! This only lasts a minute though, because the life story types are always tapping your arm, or saying 'you know?' to make sure you're really listening.

Lucky for her, the other woman sitting at the bus stop worked for a funeral home and explained that Potter's Field burials were only done if no one claimed the body, and not when there were different parties claiming rights to the deceased's remains. You never know who you're sitting next to. The craziest part of this experience was that when the woman got up to leave (she wasn't even waiting on a bus), I noticed she had a brown paper bag with a Bud Light bottle sticking out the top of it. She was probably sipping it the whole time I was using my 'don't look up' strategy.

I find the most interesting life stories shared are those told by senior citizens. You can really get an education listening to them. One that sticks out is the time I ran into this cute, petite, gray-haired woman sitting at the bus stop next to her senior citizen building. We started chatting about the weather and the possibility of showers and she began to tell me about her life. She grew up in Newark, met her husband when they were both in high school, and they married and raised five children who all lived in other states now. She was finally getting used to living in the senior citizen building after burying her husband five years ago. She didn't care to move in with her children because they would fuss too much and treat her like a child. She was finally learning to enjoy herself, adjust to being alone and independent, and had made a couple of friends in the building.

Now this, is my kinda life story. I even let a couple of buses pass me by (she was just sitting outside and not waiting for a bus) because I didn't want to interrupt her. Truth be told, I really don't mind listening to any of these life stories. I've always been fascinated by the various paths people travel in life. Some of them are life-affirming and others are precautionary tales. In the end, I suppose it all unfolds the way the Lord originally intended, centuries before we were born.

I should note that bus stop shenanigans border moreso on the bizarre, bold and odd than on the dangerous. For example, I went to discard something in the trashcan while waiting on a bus and as I approached it, a lady standing nearby suddenly picked it up, turned it over and proceeded to use it like a desk. I kid you not. She rested her pocketbook on top of it, burrowed through her bag to find a sandwich and proceeded to eat it. I must've caught ten different species of insects when my mouth dropped open in disbelief. Even more bizarre , though was her next move . She got on the bus, paid her fare and then went to the back door, and exited the bus before it pulled off. Extremely bizarre!

Another time, I encountered a woman slurping the meat so loudly off of a chicken wing, that I almost didn't hear the bus pull up. Yes, it was THAT loud. It was no coincidence I surmised, that a thick scent of cannabis was coming from the building behind the bus stop. The odor was thick and rivaled the scent of the incense used in my Episcopal church during the Resurrection season. I think the chicken wing broad had a case of the munchies via a contact. Yowza!

Lastly, there is something about a bus stop that makes everyone feel like an undiscovered sensation. I cannot count how many times I have been treated to aging rappers, crooners and other would-be superstars. Sadly, most of them are lacking in any real talent, and others are lacking in reality and honest self-assessment skills: The misguided fellow about to hop the bus, rapping "Countin' all my benjamins; stackin' all my benjamins." If he had That many benjamins, would he be riding the bus? The gray-haired gentleman coasting up to me on a bicycle trying to win my affection crooning some old school R&B. His mouth was open just wide enough to count the remaining 10 teeth he possessed.

These are all true stories folks (and maybe some loosely based on actual incidents). I don't offer them as negative testimony of the transit experience. I simply impart them to give you the full picture, should you ever find yourself waiting to ride Satan's station wagons.

CHAPTER 6 – BUS DRIVER DRAMA

Now, we come to those at the helm of these wonderful transit machines. The bus drivers. I remember as a child, being very excited to get on the bus and smiling happily at the driver, thinking her or she was so cool. I liked their uniforms and they seemed so powerful, maneuvering such a huge vehicle with that large steering wheel. I was amazed at how they navigated the tricky turns and missed hitting parked cars. Despite all their power, they seemed to be nice, smiling and friendly.

Well, things have changed! It is rare that you see a bus driver smiling. Very few are friendly or nice, and a good number of them don't drive well at all. This change may be due in part to the whackadoodles they have to deal with on a daily basis but if you ask me, a decent percentage of those commandeering our sacred chariots are a few stops short of a zone. And boy are they mean!

Case in point, we all know of the cheerful little tykes that board the bus and get such a thrill grabbing the long line of fare receipt tickets off the fare box. The glee that these little cuties feel is contagious and one of the more pleasant things one experiences on the bus. Apparently, many of the drivers are immune to this joy. They glare at the kid and tell them to 'keep it moving', or give the parent a look that says 'control your child'. Perhaps worst of all, they snatch the ticket train before the youngster has a chance to. Now, how cruel is that! What does it hurt them anyway? What manner of beast would deprive these innocents of the fun that is paper receipts? Who does that?! The meanie bus drivers, that's who!

If it's any consolation, today's drivers are equal opportunity meanies – kids, seniors, handicapped, pregnant, whoever. They are sometimes so unnecessarily rude and abrupt. I am of the mind that some of them are on a serious power trip. Perhaps the only power they have in their lives is when they put on that uniform and take their seat behind the big, bad steering wheel. I could be wrong, but I don't think so…

For instance, it used to be you board the bus and are putting your fare in the box and the driver would politely say "Ma'am or Sir, the law prohibits me from moving the bus until you are standing behind the white line." Yes, the dreaded white line. Didn't even matter if the bus was packed. He couldn't move until all were behind it or the world would come to an end, I guess. NOW, they could care less about that white line and all politeness is a relic of the past. When they're ready to take off, to catch a light or whatever, they hit the gas. You could have one foot on a step and the other up on the floor of the bus and vroom, they're off! You can wind up on the floor or in another passenger's lap (almost never a pleasant experience, but stay focused). All of a sudden they have a reckless need for speed. What's that all about?! A power trip, that's what! They do it because they can.

Another way these hokey helmsmen and women flex their muscles is their use of the brakes. How on earth did some of these drivers pass the road test? I fear a re-test is in order for about 50% of today's drivers. When they approach a red light, you would think they would press gradually on the brake and bring the bus to a smooth stop. Not the case! It is actually a stomach-lurching, neck-snapping, lunch-losing affair. They brake abruptly, then release it, break abruptly again, release again and on and on. I once counted a driver doing it seven times before coming to a complete stop and by then, the light was green.

Who does that?! A power-tripping whacko who needs their license revoked, that's who!

Drivers also let you know who's the boss by determining where they stop to pick you up (or drop you off). After all the trouble somebody must've gone to to put up those cutesy signs that let the public know where the bus stops, it turns out it was a complete waste of time and money. Where the bus actually stops is under the complete control of the driver. It can be a couple of feet before the stop, or a few feet after the stop. I'm talking about when there's no traffic backup that would force them to ignore the designated transit stop area. They simply do not feel like adhering to their own established practices.

Believe it or not, drivers seem most agitated when approaching a crowded bus stop. You would think they would be happy to get as many customers as possible, but it's not the case. They purposely drive either beyond the crowd or a few feet before the stop, forcing the riders to have to walk up or back to board the bus. You should see the little dance and jockeying for position the riders engage in when trying to determine exactly where the bus will stop. Sometimes, they don't stop at all angering the departing rider, claiming the rider didn't press the buzzer in time. Perhaps they should slow down if they're going so fast that they can't even stop. The brakes obviously work well, so what's the problem?

I've had this very thing happen to me more times than I can count and usually when the weather is bad. The drivers' attitudes need serious adjustment. One time, I pressed the buzzer well before the stop and we even caught a red light before my stop. Do you know when the light turned green, she rode right past my stop?! Despite my angry "HEY, THIS IS MY STOP!" she proceeded two blocks up to the next stop. Originally, I intended to exit via the back door, but I decided that I needed to give her a piece of my mind. I was so ready to unleash all manner of profanity upon this wicked woman, but one of the passengers was an older woman I had just been chatting with at the bus stop. Instead, I calmly walked to the front, looked her dead in the eye and said "Thank you so much. I'll be sure to vote for you for bus driver of the year." I don't know if I mentioned this before, but biting sarcasm is another one of my gifts.

Unfortunately, another way these meanies make it clear who's controlling the chariot is by making you wait before they decide to open the door to let you out. It is pretty hard to walk off the bus in a huff when the driver takes their sweet time opening the door. You stand there waiting for what seems like an eternity, and then turn around and look at them in time enough to catch them smiling, before they finally let you off. They are a sinister and sadistic lot, I tell you! You give them a look that says "Hello, moron! Open the door!", but the reality of the situation is that you must beg these power-trippers to let you out. In the interest of full disclosure, I must admit that I did call that driver a choice phrase that would be most inappropriate in a classroom or church, but she asked for it. They push me to the brink and it ain't riiiight-TA! I mean, who does that?! A power junkie, desperate for relevancy, that's who!

Another driver tactic that triggers my bus rage is when the goon behind the wheel doesn't open the back door. I know they see me because like I said, I'm a planner and I stand up a full stop early so I don't wind up injured when they break umpteen times. Smart, right? Nope. First they get mad, because they think I'm getting off. But I indicate with my face, 'Duh. No! I want the next stop, you idiot!' My planning is all for naught however, because when he gets to my stop to let some other passengers on, he fails to open the back door.

I try to remain calm and say in a pleasant voice "Back Door". It's loud enough for him to hear, but still my inside voice. Nothing. This, even though I see him glancing at me via that mirror by the back door. So, I use my outside voice, which is louder, but still calm and polite. He ignores me again and eventually the whole bus is screaming "BACK DOOR!" because they've all been through it before. Do you know that this moron got ready to pull off? It was then that I was forced to use my 'in the midst of a crowd on New Year's eve' voice (which is loud enough for the dead, the undead and even Jesus Christ Himself to hear) and I growled "BACK DOOR!!!"

Do you know this shady, trifling, game-playing driver had the nerve to have an attitude?! Even worse, some of my bus riding comrades turned on me and looked at me judgmentally for yelling like a maniac to get off the bus. I saw it as a potential false imprisonment situation, while they thought I was a TADD. What ever happened to sticking together, people?! So frustrating. You just can't win with these power-tripping imbeciles.

Another pet peeve I have with these pretentious pilots of public service is their unwillingness to answer the simplest of questions, coupled with their flat-out mean spiritedness in giving out the wrong information on purpose. They assume people ride buses every day and know all the fare information and regulations of the transit system. Well, sometimes special situations and circumstances arise. Buscard holders may be without their buscard that day and have no clue how much money is required zone to zone. Someone's car may've broken down, forcing them to hop the bus until it's fixed. God forbid you ask, how much from point A to point B? Or, where does the zone end? What planet do these drivers come from? They look at you like you are the stupidest fool riding the bus. Some of them assume you're one of those trifling riders that's up to no good. Just answer the question, buddy. Boggles the mind.

One morning on my way to a new tutorial case, I wanted to get off a block before where I regularly stop because it was closer to the new case address, so I ask the driver "Is there a stop before Grove and Central?" She points angrily indicating that Grove and Central is up there. I was angry, too.

My knee was sore and I was not in the mood and I told her that's not what I asked you. She ignored me and just sped past the stop to Grove and Central. She received a few choice words as I exited and trudged my way back a block and a half, only to see another bus on the same line stop exactly at the spot I asked my driver about. I was livid and limping. I didn't make up these stops. Your bosses did. So much unnecessary anger, directed at the wrong ones. How about you fix your face, answer simple questions and pretend you're happy to have this job. Shhhheeesh!

See, I don't like to be ornery and contentious, but they force my hand! I'm still having trouble understanding how I can board a bus with a 2-zone buscard at Point A to go to the mall (Point B) and not have to put in any additional money and yet, on the return trip to the same Point A, they want 75 cents more. Exactly, how does that work? It's the same distance. I mean, I'm a math tutor and used to teach Social Studies including those 'estimate the distance on the map' type questions. It seems pretty simple. Whenever I ask a driver to explain that, all I get is attitude and usually , "I don't know about that, but if you want to ride past here, I need 75 cents more!" Well, even if there is messy weather, I get off the bus because I refuse to be shaken down by an already overpriced transit system. Two plus two still equals four, and maybe they failed Social Studies in school, but I refuse to give them one extra dime! Principle!

Now, here's something you should know. I have done some self-reflection and realized that I am getting into more and more verbal sparring matches and 'philosophical discussions' with these 'public servants'. If you recall, at the outset I envisioned this whole bus riding thingy as some sort of joyful dalliance or Shenandoah, Shangri-la groovy, trippy type of experience. How on earth did it become a blood-pressure raising fiasco?! I think the transit powers that be should change their 'public service' theme or slogan. It is long overdue. In fact, I have a few suggestions:

1) Perhaps, 'Board at your own risk, with zero expectations of comfort, safety, convenience or pleasure.
2) Read our "Transit Practices" manual three times before you even think about asking a stupid question (please note that we consider ALL questions stupid).
3) We are doing you a favor by letting you pay excessive fares to ride our deathtraps, so

please leave all attitudes and common sense at home.

They can even end it with ENJOY YOUR RIDE or THANKS FOR RIDING TRANSIT. I should mention that not all drivers are miserable folks. I actually have favorites on each line. However, too many seem to act as if they are unhappy. Things may never get back to the kumbaya experience I had as a child, but a little bit of civility, patience and a pleasant smile go a long way. That's all I'm saying.

CHAPTER 7 – TRANSIT TOMFOOLERY

In everyday life, we encounter miscellaneous realities and situations over which we have little or no control. These things are annoying, infuriating and nonsensical but we must tolerate them because it is simply out of our hands. We have no choice whatsoever in the matter. The same is true with transit commuter life. The average rider is faced with an insufferable amount of tomfoolery on a daily basis. These confounding conditions would drive the average human to sheer madness, but we are not average. We are transit riders. We are thick-skinned. We are survivors. And so, we muddle through the muck and mire that is daily transit life, often overcoming the unthinkable. I may have alluded to some of this earlier, but let me explain because it bears repeating.

One of my biggest issues on the bus is spacing. There are simple levels of decency that must be maintained at all costs. I've made a lot of progress with sharing part of my seat with someone who is not being honest in judging how much of their neighbor's space they covet. I realize that we all come in varying shapes and sizes, and that's cool. We really should be more patient and understanding with one another.

BUT, why is it that when I'm on a bus that is virtually empty (just me and maybe two other passengers all spread out), someone boards and sits right behind or in front of me? RIGHT behind me! WHY?!! Are they lonely? Are they frightened? Are they stalkers? There are 28 or more other seats that could've been selected and they decide to enter MY area?? I know it seems a bit much to claim areas on a public bus, but I was here first, doggonit! If you're that desperate or lonely, get a pet...or a toy...or something. Anything! Just get away from me! Wars have been declared over far less uncivilized behavior. Who does that?! It is inexcusable tomfoolery.

Another thing that's always bothered me is the fact that there are no passenger seatbelts on public buses. If I'm not mistaken, the driver has a seatbelt. So why not the passengers? (especially considering how today's drivers drive). Do you mean to say they care so little for the riders who are keeping them in business that they neglect to ensure their safety when placing them in the hands of some of the ill-trained, maniacal menaces that they hire? Frankly, this is a smack in the face and a huge oversight. Now that I think about it, they don't even go over the use of the emergency doors like they do on airplanes. I'm starting to feel some kinda way.

I must admit that more often than not, it is my fellow passengers who are a major source of angst. One of the unavoidable issues I have with them is scent. Some folks apparently empty their entire bottle of cologne or perfume before boarding the bus. They know very well they will be on here with other people and obviously could care less who might be offended, irritated, overwhelmed or asphyxiated by their felonious fumes. Do they have a date? Trying for a promotion? Trying to cover up even worse body odor? What?! They need to cut it out!

What gets me is that you can't tell them they don't smell good. They board the bus like they have Arrived. They take their seat like the person sitting next to them has just gotten the best prize behind Door #2. In their feeble minds, they actually believe folks are envious and jealous of them. The fact that not one person says 'What's that you're wearing?' or 'You smell good' doesn't faze them one bit. Nope, this malodorous moron doesn't realize there's a direct link to his or her cologne and the poor sap hacking, coughing and convulsing nearby. I implore anyone who is guilty of this to cease and desist, immediately. PLEASE! Countless souls, noses and the EPA will be forever grateful.

This next situation is of a very delicate and sensitive nature, but bear with me. Apparently, the buses are a magnet for the well-endowed. I kid you not. There is an outbreak of males who are riding the public buses who are equipped to ensure the continuation of the species. Why do I say this? Well, whenever I sit next to a male (tall, short, skinny, thick, heavy), more often than not, he is sitting with his legs and feet at least twelve inches or more apart. This leads to them taking up a sizeable portion of my seat and now, we have a problem.

I have never asked but I'm guessing they sit this way because were they to move their feet or legs the slightest bit closer together, they might smash and do irreversible damage to their ample personage. This is all theory of course and I admit that I am tempted to glance downward to confirm anaconda or garter snake status, but then I'd have those judgmental older women and church folk on my back again. No avoiding them, that's for sure.

In any event, I have prepared a speech should the situation of limited space for me, become any more intolerable than it already is. It goes something like this… "My good man. I am extremely pleased that the good Lord has seen fit to bless you in your loinage, but seeing as you paid for just one seat and not 1 ½ seats to accommodate your massive essence, do you think you can employ some of those scoop and shift maneuvers you've been using since childhood, so that I may fully enjoy the seat that I have paid for?" It is just unbelievable, in more ways than one I might add. Hopefully, I will never have to recite this speech, but I do what I can for the sake of all riders, and I am ready.

Moving on, most riders are painfully aware of the wanton waste that goes on daily in the transit world. What do I mean? Well, our fares could be reduced significantly if they would stop putting up those signs and pictures of things that are forbidden on the bus. They should save their money and perhaps go with one sign that says "Just do whatever you want!" because no one, including the drivers, pays attention to them.

NO FOOD OR DRINK. That's laughable. People board the bus eating and drinking (not just soft drinks either). I've even seen drivers have someone meet them at a stop and hand them food, which they eat while driving. They don't even wait for red lights or stops. This sets a very bad example for the passengers. How can you tell them not to eat, when you are eating? You can't! Not to mention, nobody follows the rule we learned in grade school – if you don't have enough for everyone, you can't eat it. The flipside is when they bring out something that smells awful and robs you of your appetite for hours, even days. Just rude and no manners. They chomp loudly, talk while they're eating and are just generally uncouth and ill-mannered. Barbarians, I tell ya.

NO LOUD MUSIC. Sure, sure. What is it about the word 'loud' that people are not understanding? Remember when youngsters walked around carrying those large boombox radios wherever they went – school, park, church? Thank goodness today's youth don't like carrying anything extra (including their school books sometimes, but I digress) or we'd be in big trouble. Well, they may as well be carrying the boomboxes because that's how loud their ipod and phone music tends to be. Feels like you're in the front row at a rock concert or something, and quite frankly, I don't always like their music choices. True, some adults are guilty of this excessive volume as well, but for crying out loud – Read the signs! Tragically, the music you are forced to hear or listen to on the public buses is, more often than not, tantamount (nice, right?) to an assault on the ears. A felonious, aggravated assault. People blast the most juvenile, non-melodic, vile nursery rhyme type, profane crap you've ever heard in your life. These folks are gonna be deaf! Oh sure. Share your music, but not your food. So unfair.

NO CELLPHONE USAGE. Hahahahahaha! Yeah, right! This has become the most annoying nuisance to ever plague modern society. Using cell phones in public places. Sure, it seemed like a good idea at the start. I mean, I'm a huge Trekkie and I thought the communicators were cool, even though they were on speaker mode so we could hear the conversation in the episodes. Today, however, folks are not even in speakerphone mode, but you can still hear the entire conversation. Unacceptable! Volume control, people. Volume control!

I don't know about you, but I don't want to be privy to every sordid detail of your life. I don't wanna know your business. I don't need to know

you're playing hooky, or you're overdo for your
monthly visit, or the GYN called you for a follow-
up visit. I don't want to know that you're using
part of your rent money to upgrade your cell phone
and get a manicure or pedicure. I don't wanna
hear about how the pedicurist was grossed out by
your Flintstone feet (I'm grossed out too, by the
way). Why would anyone on that bus need to
know that your husband might be sleeping with
your mother? Enough is enough. This situation is
out of control.

I also don't want to hear a play-by-play of your
ride and neither should the person on the other end
of the phone. Someone who needs to know
exactly where you are while you're riding the bus
is exhibiting extremely controlling behavior. Get
rid of them.

Nevertheless, I hear things like, "Yeah, I'm
almost there…No, we're still on Central Ave…No,
not that part of Central Ave…No, I don't see a
carwash…Oh, remember that green car Mookie
used to drive…No, not that one, the red
G.T.O….no, not the Mookie from 15th St…Mookie
from down the hill…Slim's half brother…No, not
that Slim, the one that got A.J. pregnant…No, not
light-skinned A.J., brown-skinned A.J…Yeah, dat

one…You didn't know Mookie and Slim didn't have the same father?…What! Everybody know dat…Wait, I don't see no Dunkin Donuts…Hold on. "Excuse me driver, is this the 24?"…Listen, I'mma call you back. I got on a 94 instead of a 24!"

I kid you not. I hear these type of conversations and worse all the time. They might need to consider 'cell phone only' buses and 'no cell phones allowed' buses. It's just too much!

One last situation riders are forced to deal with is the fact that the buses have become mobile flea markets. And business is BOOMING. People will try to sell you any and everything on the bus or at the bus stop. If it's payday for you, you might need to avoid the buses altogether because their sales pitch is pretty convincing. They sell socks, cigarettes, clocks, watches, CDs, DVDs, hats, notebooks, makeup, candy, fake buscards, bootleg movies, pocketbooks, phones, jeans, other clothes and even household appliances. One guy had a coffeemaker, unopened and in its original box, talking about, "I just need $5 for this. It's a steal, y'all." Truer words were never spoken!

There are countless other things that a bus rider must endure but they are far too numerous , sordid and disturbing to go into in great detail (perhaps in another book, wink wink). The bottom line is that we who participate in this transit circus are not punks. No, far from it. We are witnesses to things that are barbaric, unseemly, unsightly, immoral and occasionally illegal. We are forced to keep a stiff upper lip about it however, if we expect to arrive at our destinations in one piece and unscathed. The truth of the matter is that we are very scathed. We are traumatized for life, but does anyone care? Probably not...

CHAPTER 8 – YOU SHOULD STILL RIDE

Most people reading this book would automatically assume that I am advising you to avoid riding public buses at all costs. Not at all. I am actually a great fan of public transportation, believe it or not. I ride buses and trains interstate and intrastate all the time. I also ride subways in New York and Washington, D.C. So, by all means, treat yourself to a few bus rides in your lifetime. Hear me out...

First of all, the bus is often the best option for traveling to places that are very tricky to get to by car. There are also some places that even the GPS can't find, but the bus can. Some of these places are so remote, that it is actually best to travel by bus so that you have a bunch of witnesses should you ever disappear (I watch a lot of forensic tv shows). Bus riders are the nosiest folks on the planet and will remember every little detail about you (sock color, phone case, missing teeth). There will at least be a trail for the investigative authorities to follow. Worst case scenario, they will be able to ascertain your time of death with more accuracy.

Secondly, I can say without hesitation that the bus riding experience prepares individuals on a level similar to that of FBI or CIA training. You analyze, decipher and suppress massive amounts of information on a daily basis. You know when to see and when not to see. You know what to say and what not to say. You understand all things confidential and top secret. You can probably get some high-level, government security clearance job based on your bus adventures. In fact, I'd even venture to say that you are probably better prepared than most to face Armageddon or the apocalypse or any of those other inevitable catastrophic events that start with an 'A'.

Riding the bus is also a good way to waste time and I mean this in a good way. If your intention is to be late, the public bus route is the answer for you. I mean, I have been known to get perfect connections for three different lines on more than one occasion, but there are some kinks to be worked out timewise. More often than not, you will be waiting – for the bus to arrive, for slow boarders, for heavy traffic slowing things down, for a slow bus driver, for a fast bus driver who makes you miss or wait longer for your connecting bus.

Despite all this waiting, there is a bright side. You can get a lot of stuff done. You can check emails that have piled up, play games on your phone, become more familiar with a new phone, catch up on social media, listen to your ipod, read books (hint hint) and use all those other expensive gadgets you buy but never get a chance to fully use and enjoy. I'm just saying.

I could go on, but Transit isn't paying me for PR work (and certainly not after this book). Perhaps the best reason for riding the bus (besides absolute necessity) is that it is one of the best places to observe and interact with people. Yes, I gripe about people being nosey, but I am just as nosey as the next person. I prefer to call it being observant. We never really stray too far from our early roots, do we?

The fact of the matter is that I love people, or people-watching. I watch and stare at people. I get amused, startled and frightened by people. I am amazed and choked up by people's actions and interactions. I am more often than not, genuinely moved by many of the things and encounters I witness and experience during my rides. The lessons I learn about humanity are priceless, and for usually less than five dollars, I have a front row

seat and access to the laboratory of life. It is
Reality TV in a sense, sans the cameras. Doesn't
get any better than that…

THANK YOU SO MUCH FOR READING!
You are officially TCers (transit chroniclers).
GOD BLESS YOU! THAT IS ALL….Or is it???

ACKNOWLEDGEMENTS

I must first acknowledge GOD. It is only because of HIS mercy, grace, love and favor that I was able to write this book. My gifts, such that they are, came from GOD. I am a Christian and not at all ashamed to praise, glorify and magnify HIS significance in my life. In no way, do I offer this testimony to offend or exclude anyone. On the contrary, I have great respect for anyone who relies heavily on their faith and the belief in a higher power. But I am a Christian and my Lord and Savior is JESUS CHRIST.

Next, I am forever indebted to my family for all the love, patience, kindness, truthfulness and generosity they have shown me all of my life. The past couple of years of adjustment have been trying and without my family, especially my twin sister, AUDREY BROWN-GIVENS, my cuz aka the triplet, JUDITH COMPTON, my young cuz and 'dista' JASMINE BRAY-WILLIAMS and my uncle ROBERT V. SMITH, I may very well have been homeless. We are all essentially a job, paycheck, situation, attitude or misunderstanding away from homelessness. Family is family, yes but you didn't have to, and you did. Eternal gratitude & LOVE!

I also want to give SPECIAL THANKS to my beautiful mother, CAROLYN BROWN who teaches me patience, humility and unconditional love. To my brother MELVIN BROWN, Jr. My HERO. He's taught me what courage through service to country and patriotism means and to follow my passions. To my beautiful, namesake niece, CHANEL ANITA GIVENS who makes me feel such joy and teachers me that there is indeed, hope for the future. And THANKS to my cousins FLORENCE and TOMMY HATCHETT, my Auntie CAROLYN MILLS DILL and my cousin WENDY MILLS STANLEY and many other family too numerous to name unfortunately, but ALL OF YOU keep me encouraged, confident and feeling loved. LOVE y'all.

I must thank my author cousins HILLARY ROY & KIM KIRKLEY and my buddy WILLIAM "Mike" BARBEE, for sharing their expertise in writing books. LOVE y'all.

I also thank my friend COLEEN TOEWS, who literally kept me afloat at the beginning of this adjustment period. My lean years became my LEEN years for a time and I will never forget you for that, my vmm/dmmt4l.

I also thank a very special FOREVER FRIEND, RIC ROSS who has always been in my corner and always checks up on me. We initially met due to a mutual admiration for the artistry of Frank Sinatra, but our forever friendship was forged through loss, promises to angels (his special rose and sweet angel JUDI), heartache and growth. The best is truly yet to come for both of us, my friend. LOVE and eternal TUESDAY HUGS to you.

SPECIAL THANKS also to some other offline, lifelong friends including, but not limited to MONICA ANICITO, GENENE BELL & JAMES CALLENDAR. Lotsa LOVE to you guys, who are more like FAMILY.

I also need to thank some online friends, some whom I've met and others who I've never met and yet it seems I've known them all my life. HUGE THANKS to my Voicer Pallies especially RICK APT, BEVERLY ELANDER, CAROL & BRAD LoRICCO, ANNETTE RUSSO, ANTHONY DiFLORIO III, PB ED WALTERS, LEO SCANLON, MARK PETTY, MIKE BROCKMAN, VIN REDA, EILEEN CRAFFEY, the late SANDY IRWIN and his beautiful wife JUDY. Eternal THANKS to PHYLLIS TALISMAN (my southern SoFLA twinnie, now Angel) and my buddy, KATHY MANNS (my author friend who penned a wonderful ode to my Nana).

I want to shout out my Texas Fam, KELLI and KAMILLE NUNEZ and their sweet Angel, MAMA KAREN. They have also been in my corner for a long time now. Love you guys.

Have to say THANK YOU to my FLUNGER buddies. It's a long story, but suffice it to say we've been kicked out of better places, but it all worked out for the best in the end. KIMMI (Poof) SEGER, CINDI (OK via SI) SCHEUERMAN, LYNDA (sib) LARMORE, CINDY (Oh, Canada) DESCHAMPS and to my Cally Pallies, JOANNA HOLMES & BILL KUHN.

I want to thank another Facebook friend who I feel like I've known forever. LEA MacNAMARA. Thanks & GOD BLESS YOU (but still no threading). All of my facebook friends were my true sounding board for this book. BLESS YOU!

My other online friends are fellow fans of Bebe Winans. They just get him, like I do. God Bless you, SHEILA KNIGHT and BRANDI HILL. You've been a huge inspiration and your encouragement means a lot to me. Also need to shout out Mr. Winans' personal assistant, TONI 'TClass' LEWIS. She is my sister from another mister and inspired me to start working out, among other things. She's a sweet but no-nonsense type of chick with a heart of gold. LOVE my Beebs' Peeps. Of course I have to thank the one and only BEBE WINANS. Singer, songwriter, producer, author, Christian, you name it. I have been greatly inspired by this dude's work, faith and joyful nature. As he would say 'Thank Ya, Sir!" Oh, do yourself a favor and go get The THREE WINANS BROTHERS' (3WB) uplifting CD "FOREIGN LAND".

I know this is getting long, but I have more... My classmates from JUNIOR HS, SCOTT HS, SHU and Rutgers Law School. They include DOMITA WHITE (who did much more to bring me out of my shell to embrace my wacky side than she knows), DAWN ROSS, KATHLEEN McDONALD, ROLAND BEVAN, JANICE RAMSAY, NANCY HENDERSON, LETITIA WALDEN, SONYA EVANS, ROSEMARIE FOX, DAWN MARABLE-FIELDS, CHRISTOPHER REGAN, LEROY F. BENNETT, DENNIS 'Dimpz' McCALL, CONNIE 'Hi CON' MONTALVO & GILEN CHAN. LOVE each of you for being a friend and not changing or outgrowing me (smile) as the years piled up.

I want to thank three ladies who I consider my SISTERS IN CHRIST. They are GALE BENNETT, KIM ROYSTER & my new buddy MIB (smile). You ladies do more than you know to keep me on the Christian path and I am so very grateful for that. AMEN. Bless you always. Love you much.

Professionally, I'd like to thank two people who believed in me and gave me a chance. JEROLINE CHAMBERS who I love and miss. She was my guidance counselor and friend from high school until her last days on this earth. I also owe much gratitude to DR. KENNETH KING who gave me a chance and believed in my ability to not only teach, but to mentor. THANK YOU! I thank ALL of my teaching colleagues. The educational trenches are just as trying, albeit far more rewarding in the end, as the transit trenches. Praying for you guys ALWAYS.

I also owe want to thank the EAST ORANGE SCHOOL DISTRICT for giving me the opportunity to educate and enlighten my wonderful students. To my many STUDENTS and TUTEES over the years, you have ALL taught me far more than I could ever teach you. Thank You!

THANKS to my neighbors - Schuyler Terrace, Burchard and Washington St, STAND UP! Rough at times, but every experience toughened me up for the life I now live. 'Preciate y'all – Hoffmans, Elliots, Colemans, Pattersons, Williamses, Peoples, Darbys, Whites, Simpsons, Hendersons, Blakes, Humphreys, Stams, other Hoffmans, Dixons, Washingtons and Wards. We made it out and up!

I, of course, must thank my Brothers and Sisters in TRANSIT. We have been through so much together (passengers and drivers) and we earn our stripes each and every time we climb those stairs and ride to and fro.

FINALLY, I thank my SWEET ANGEL, my grandmother NANA. My twin sister and I were born on the 52nd birthday of HAZEL CHARLOTTE ROY SMITH and for 40 years we were blessed to benefit from her wisdom, example, sacrifice and unconditional love. In my darkest hours, I hear the quiet, gentle flapping of her angel wings & I know that I'll be fine. THANK YOU, NANA! I am who I am because of you and I LOVE YOU for all eternity. As I have always said, I don't owe you anything; I OWE YOU EVERYTHING!!!

ABOUT THE AUTHOR

Anita Brown, born to parents Carolyn and the late Melvin Brown, Sr., and raised by grandmother (NANA) Hazel Charlotte Roy Smith, is a lifelong resident of East Orange, New Jersey. She considers herself the middle child because she has an older brother, Melvin Jr. and she was born four minutes before her fraternal twin sister, Audrey Brown-Givens. Anita is passionate about sports, music and Star Trek among other things, but she has always enjoyed writing. Her earliest recollection of writing is a poem she wrote at a family gathering for her great Aunt Mary Kirkley's birthday. However, a middle school friend, Domita White, recently reminded her that she once wrote a funny poem about a sock and a creative story based on Aesop's Fables in 8th grade. She has been writing ever since, about various topics in various forms including poetry, short stories, songs, song parodies, newspaper editorials, and on blogs and websites. Anita has written more than 70 poems and songs, and occasionally recites at poetry venues.

www.ingramcontent.com/pod-product-compliance
Lightning Source LLC
Chambersburg PA
CBHW062023040426
42447CB00010B/2117